You Are Not Your Story

Lenieka Brown

You Are Not Your Story

As a writer, I wanted to keep these stories very short. I hope that they touch the hearts and lives of each person that reads them. I have included a special place in this book just for you to share your story. Special thanks to my loving brothers Darian Ford and Richard Jackson for walking me through this process each step of the way.

Contents

Chapter 1. Unidentified Man

Chapter 2. The Yellow Jacket

Chapter 3. Silky Velvet

Chapter 4. Dope Boy Blues

Helpful Numbers

YOU ARE NOT YOUR STORY

Unidentified Man

I heard a loud noise coming from my kitchen as I laid on the bed hesitating on moving. Slowly, I emerged from my bed to see what all the commotions was. The blinds were on the floor. I had left my window open because a mouse had gotten caught in the refrigerator motor. I quickly closed the window, picked up the blinds and proceeded to head back to bed, only to be awakened by an unidentified man choking me.

I yelled Stacey stop playing, get your hands off me, your hurting me the more I screamed the harder his embrace became. That is the moment that I realized that this was not the man that I had shared my life with; it was a total stranger. I could feel myself slipping in and out of consciousness as the cold blade of the knife pressed up against my neck. I stopped!!!! My son had been awakened. I looked at my son with tears in my eyes my life was flashing before me. I decided that I would live that day and begin to obey his every command.

Thoughts raced through my head as he stood over me. He had on a stocking cap and a ski mask on with one eye cut out of it, with his bottoms already off. How long was he standing there before he decided to attack me pondered my brain. He begins to climb on top of me, in my small still voice I asked him would he please wear a condom because I had just had an abortion and I didn't want to get pregnant by someone that I didn't know. He ignored me and forced himself inside of me. Seconds turned into minutes; minutes turned into hours. It seemed like time

 had just frozen. I was at a complete standstill. My soul had left my body, and I was no longer there, my eyes gazed over at my son, and he looked very puzzled at me and then smiled. Who was this man and where on earth did he come from?

I begin to think back to every person that I had encountered, and his voice did not ring a bell. This man must be crazy; he is trying to make love to a person that he is raping. Rage began to set in my heart. How dare you violate me while my 7-month-old son lay beside us watching, not to mention wake me up out of a good night's sleep talking about how good my body is to you. These words wanted to come out so badly, but I laid there in silence and just waited for the time to pass, and finally, time passed.

I could never forget how this man's slender framed body just slithered across mines like a snake in the grass. "There will be more men coming in behind me," he stated. I need you to lay here very still, Randy, Gerald, and Donald are on their way behind me. I don't want you to be afraid because they are going to penetrate your ass and masturbate in your face. He walked away, and I remained still with the covers over my head. I counted silently. One one- hundred, two one- hundred until it felt like I was running out of numbers. No one appeared. I thought to myself it's all or nothing because I was not about to let Randy and them have their way. I jumped up and begin to run. I beat on the wall of my little project apartment until I woke someone up. They came over, secured the apartment and called the police.

My feelings were all over the place I couldn't believe that this just happened to me, out of all people. Police were everywhere. Everything became so distant as I rode away in the back of the ambulance with my child in hand. We made it to our destination and was placed inside of an exam room. The doctors came in, and the police entered and as I begin to tell my story, so much guilt had come across me like all of this was my fault. I was being paid back by the lord with this bad luck because I had broken one of the ten commandments. Thou should not kill just pounced through my head. If only I had not had this abortion and let this child live I wouldn't be going through all this hell now. Thou should not kill…only if I had not listened to him when he told me that he didn't want any more children. Thou shall not kill, thou shall not kill, thou shall not kill. played on and on and on for hours. The father of the aborted child appeared, so I begin to scream and blame him. Only if you hadn't left me there by myself, you were too busy trying to rush home to take her to work. The more I yelled at him, the lower he began to sink into the chair.

The guilt that I harbored instantly transferred to him. He didn't say or mumble a word. I tried to live my life as healthy as I could, but it was very hard everyone was a suspect to me. Over the next couple of months, I begin to move, walk, and talk differently. I wore turtlenecks in the summer, slept in the day and stayed up all night waiting for the unidentified man to come. In my mind, I had murdered him a thousand times and several different ways. I wanted so bad just to pull the trigger and make him feel like I had felt while he was bumping and grinding on top of me to the crazy rhythm of his mind. I became a prisoner in my own body, and no matter how hard I tried I just could not break free. Life just stopped for me and all of the feelings that I once possessed disappeared. I told myself repeatedly you cannot keep living like this. You got to come out of this shell, but as the sunset and the moon rose I sunk deeper into a pit. I begin to wear a mask, letting nothing or no one in. How could someone so beautiful be in this type of condition.? One day as I laid on the couch the phone rang, and to my surprise, it was the detective that had been working my case. How are you doing, and I replied with I am well under the circumstances? She said we have finally caught the bastard how fast can you come down to the station. I replied I would be there in 20 minutes.

Upon arriving at the station, I became scared each step that I took felt like I was sinking into quicksand, my legs grew numb as my heart skipped several beats. She was waiting for me at the front entrance with his id. She asked me have I ever seen this man before and I told her no. We found him downtown drilling holes into a women's bathroom the outside of the house with a drill. She heard the noise and called the police. He was caught with a bag full of tools and the hat and stocking cap in the bag. Is this the cap that you remember seeing? I stated yes, it is I turned to her, and I begin to cry; she said I told you that I would find him. She then starts to tell me that there were other women and that he was a serial rapist and I was lucky to be alive. He had been watching you for a whole year hiding in the bushes of the abandoned house across the street from yours. He even would watch you with a flashlight through your window while you slept. I looked at her and said this bastard is crazy. Who in their right mind behaves like this. Only a monster could do these things. As these words came out of my mouth, they released me from everything that I was feeling deep down inside.

I turned towards the door and grabbed the handle to leave, and she handed me some papers I asked what this is. These are your attacker's test results; he is HIV positive. My heart sank deep down into the pit of my stomach. Every emotion that I had ever felt rose again, but this time the pain was ten times worse. I yelled how can I escape such turmoil. The same knife that he placed against my neck was now embedded in my flesh.

This man had a hold of my mind even though he had been captured. I was lifeless in a body that didn't belong to me, but to my oppressor. Every inch I gained was stolen away from me once again. I walked out the station numb; nothing even mattered to me anymore not even life. I stepped off of the curb into traffic and was almost hit by a car. I never looked up or missed a beat. How am I going to tell the people that I had been intimate with that I had been exposed to the HIV by the man who raped me.

All types of emotion rumbled inside of me and the things that the adults said about me were coming to pass. You are going to be just like your mom and die like her too I thought. Gin became my friend for the next couple of hours. It drowned out all the pain long enough for me to tell everybody. I was in shock because no one wanted to leave me but stay right by my side

through it all. The thought of me dying like my mother took a toll on my life I begin drinking a fifth of gin a day. One day I just snapped and said I got to pull myself together, so I started to get tested for HIV every three months and remained free from the virus 21 years later.

The Yellow Jacket

Darkness set upon the room as the man in the yellow jacket appeared. Very polite and charming, he hid behind a smile that could have fooled the very elect elite. He was a well-dressed man that carried himself with high standards but rained terror on every child that he encountered. I would never forget the day that he entered my room. The light from the door grew dim, as his shadow begin to develop the closer he moved towards me. The stench in the air became a familiar smell as it would linger for hours and sometimes days.

Slipping off his clothing, He would climb into my bed and push his naked body up against mines. Whispering in my ear, "We are going to play a game called, hide and seek." At the tender age of five, I thought that this was going to be fun and excitement grew in my heart. "There are rules to this game," he explained! Everything that we do here you must pinky swear never to tell. I reached my small hands up and our pinky fingers connected. Now take off your panties, He mumbled. Placing his rough hands against my legs and his fingers began to disappear into my Vagina.

No one ever warned me that a game of hide and seek would consist of this. As time went on the man in the yellow jacket became fonder of me and began to appear more often. Crafty he was, charming every adult in the house just to get close to me. No one ever questioned the look

in his eyes as I walked past him gracefully. No one even noticed that my innocence and been stolen by this sheep in wolves clothing.

No one even noticed that I walked differently, or that I became more distant, no one noticed anything strange or unfamiliar about my behavior. Thoughts began to race through my mind. Maybe they felt like I was going through some phase, I kept telling myself. I wonder if this is what ordinary people feel like. My birthday was coming up, and my parents had been planning a big celebration. I was turning the big six.

Every one that was somebody was invited. I never will forget the night of this party.

The adults had gotten drunk and fallen asleep. My friend and I sat in the beds talking about how much fun we just had. Suddenly, the light that had been peeking under the door grew dim. The doorknob began to turn, and the door slowly sprung open. Stunned, we hid under the covers playing like we were sleeping. The heaviness of his feet made the floor creak. The closer he drew near the louder it sounded.

Stillness sat in the room as I waited for his next move. Suddenly the covers flew off my head. He moved in closer, Hide and seek started all over again. Turning my head, my body laid motionless. You could see the white of my friends' eyes gazing through the darkness. I opened my mouth to warn him, but fear gripped me, and nothing came out. Don't make a sound or he will get you is all I wanted to say.

David had been discovered. He called out to him to come over and play with us, and he did. Explaining the rules of the game, the man in the yellow jacket began to unzip his pants and expose himself. Michael place your hands here and put your mouth there. Up and down he went. Now you come here and help him out. An hour had gone by, and he finally pleasured himself. He had taken another victim.

The life that David had known changed. He began to walk and talk just like me, but no one ever noticed. We never talked about what had happened because the experience became a way of life for us. Eventually, the man in the yellow jacket disappeared, leaving a trail of terror within our hearts and minds.

- **FORGIVE**

The key to it all is forgiveness. You must remember that sometimes when a person may cause you pain, it is only because they have experienced pain. This is what you call a learned behavior. They just do what they know how to do. Today I challenge you to look at things from this perspective, and it will help you understand why it is crucial for you to forgive them.

Silky Velvet

From the look in his eyes, I knew that today was going to bring trouble. He followed me as I slowly moved across the room. Watching me like a hawk, counting each step that I made. Snatching my phone, he asked me, "Why do you always have to be a whore"? The anger rose inside of him, as a dark shadow surround his head. He walked towards the bathroom still mumbling about how he should kill me. In an instant, he threw the phone in the toilet, unzipped his pants and pissed on it.

"Please not today Lord," I kept saying to myself. I knew in my heart not to say these things out loud because they would only cause me more trouble." Now, how bad do you want it he laughed and proceeded to walk away? I quickly ran to the toilet and stuck my hand in the urine-filled water and retrieved my phone. Praying that my device still had service, I walked into the kitchen to hide it. I could hear the sound of his feet as he stumped through the house.

They sounded like a heard of running bulls. What am I to do. Panicking I slide my slender body beside the refrigerator to take cover. The shatter of glass startled me as he had broken the gin bottle on the counter. Walking close to me he yelled, "Bitch you are going to die today." I was not ready to leave this world under these circumstances, so I begin to fight back.

He forcefully pushed me against the wall knocking the breath out of my body. I can't fall, if you fall to the ground you are dead, is all that replayed over and over in my mind. He took the

bottle and pushed it up against my chest and asked me why I shouldn't kill you today. I could kill you right now, and no one would come looking for you. Tears begin to run down my face. Don't cry now this is only the beginning of the end, as he pushed into the living room on the couch.

Stillness came over my body. Fear had taken a grip on me to the point that I stared into space. I tried hard to watch his every move without moving my eyes as he paced back and forth across the living floor. But with him being three-hundred and ten pounds, six feet four this was an arduous task to do. "Why do you make me do the things that I do," he stated. Insanity had taken over his mind. He ran and jumped on top of me.

I managed to get my feet up against his body to try and push and kick him off as he choked me. He grabbed my right leg twisted it and pushed his weight down on it. POW! You could hear the bone pop in my leg as it fell. Twisted and deformed as it laid motionless on the other. "What have you done to me," I screamed as the pain shot through my body. His eyes turned as dark as the night's sky as he raced back and forth across the floor. He threw his hands up and begin to panic as he looked at me screaming.

He placed his hands on top of his head and stopped. I begin to talk to myself in the third person, Laurie if you do not pull it together he is going to kill you. Forgetting the pain, I began to coach him through what had just happened. Everything is going to be ok. I will be ok. I will not tell anyone, just take my truck and leave, but when you get uptown call the ambulance to get me.

He grabbed the keys and raced out of the house. Whew, I made it through this, now how in the world am I going to get up and get to my phone. I had hidden it up under the refrigerator in the kitchen. Trying hard to push past the pain, I sat patiently and began to pray. Lord, please let this man call the ambulance, let him have some mercy in his heart for me. One hour later they arrived. That is the last day that I saw him.

Over the next couple of months my life as I had known it changed. The most prominent bone in my body had been broken, and a metal rod was placed in my leg. Faced with the reports of the doctors, feelings that I never known begin to arise inside of me. Angrily I gazed out of the window as I watched the sunset. Lost in my thoughts, I didn't notice that my dinner was on the table until I felt a nudge on my shoulder. Hard work had finally paid off after two months with my therapist.

I made it out of a wheelchair, to a walker, and then a cane. Loneliness had set in, so I allowed this man to re-enter my life. He caused trauma to my heart and body, but I could not stop loving him. He was like a soft grizzly bear with poison ivy paws. I walked days later after being tormented for hours and left alone for three days in a darkened space. The drama went on for three more years until I got up enough strength to move out and I never looked back.

- **DON'T REPEAT THE PATTERN**

	Sometimes it's hard for us to do something new. We always tend to go back to what is familiar to us. Whether it's a person, place, or a thing because that is all that we know to do. I challenge you today to leave the past behind you and don't repeat the pattern. It might be a little hard at first but remember it takes 21 days to break a habit. You can do this.

ASSIGNMENT

- Take a blank piece of paper, draw a line down the middle of it. At the top of it on the right side write down all the things that you seem to repeat in your life that needs to change. On the left-hand side of the paper write down everything that you can do that's good to change the cycle so that it will not be repeated. Doing this will make you aware of the negative patterns in your life

Lord,

I thank you today for the courage and the strength that you have given me to complete this journey. I know that all things are possible with you. As you take my hand and lead me along the way. I thank you that you go before me and make all the crooked roads straight, sending the people that you desire to help me along the way.

Dope Boy Blues

How did we get to this point, I thought to myself as my feet dangled in the air? Fighting to stay alive, the grip of his hands around my throat became too much to bare. My eyes begin to roll in the back of my head as my body hit the floor. Motionless, I could feel myself being lifted. Urine and feces started to spill out of me as flashbacks occurred in my mind.

It was a cold January day. The sun was at its peak, and its rays glared through my living room blinds. I had gotten off the couch to admire its beauty when I heard talking outside of my apartment door. Looking through the window, there was this tall, handsome gentleman standing there. I boldly opened the door and introduced myself. Hi, I'm Donna.

What is your name? He shyly responded, "Karson," and dropped his head. Ok, Mr. Karson here is my number hit me up sometime. Turning around I could see him staring at me as I walked away. A couple of days passed, and Karson called. Seeing his name on my caller I.D. excitement grew inside of me. Trying to play it off, I let the phone ring five times before picking it up.

Hello. May I speak with Donna. In my sexiest voice, I begin to respond, "this is she." Never in a million years would I have thought that the conversation would be so pleasant. After hours of talking, he politely asked me to dinner, and I excepted. Time went on, and we decided to become an item. Little did I know he had a woman that he had been living with for years. One day I decided to follow him. He hit the corner and pulled up to this brick two-story home. I sat cautiously at the

corner while I watched him greet this pregnant lady. They kissed and hugged and walked into the house. I was devastated. Weeks before this he stated, he didn't want any more children, so we agreed to have an abortion. Pushing past the pain, I decided just to play the cards that had been dealt and deal with it.

I was already in too far plus I didn't want to let go of the things that I had begun to experience. The trips to exotic places, spending thousands of dollars at a time. Every weekend I would spend a thousand dollars on hair, nails, and clothing. He would let me loose in the mall and buy anything that my hand would touch. The flowers, diamonds, and cars. The fame of being a dope boys girl.

All this fame and money came with a price. The more money he spent, the worse the beatings became. I was a prisoner bound and tied to this lifestyle. Hiding the bruises and black eyes behind make-up and expensive glasses. He would always say, that he never wanted to love anyone the way that he loved me. Surrounded by urine and feces, I asked myself, "Did love get us here"?

Blood flowed out of my mouth as the wind was being pushed inside of my body. My guardian angel was there assisting me. I had died and was brought back to life. I lifted my head and stared at him. It was like he had seen a ghost. He screamed, "You were just dead"! Frantically he began to run through the house gathering his things. Yelling," I got to get away from you"! "You are going to cost me my life and freedom"! Still, in my bodily fluids, I sat in a daze, as he

ran out the front door. It took me a while to get myself together. Pushing myself off the floor, I finally made it to the bathroom to get cleaned up. Glad that all of this was over. I got dolled up and carried on as if nothing had happened.

Weeks went by, and my money began to look funny. So, I called him. I had gotten accustomed to the lifestyle that I had been living. There is never going to be another man that's going to treat me the way that he does. That was the illusion that I sold myself to deal with him. Praying deep down inside hoping that things would change.

Things never changed. The beatings became more intense. After leaving the hospital with both my arms in a cast, two black eyes, and internal bleeding, I finally said enough is enough., and walked away from the dope boy blues. Never looking back.

- **KNOW YOUR WORTH**
- **I MADE YOU IN MY IMAGE AND LIKENESS**

Sometimes it is so easy to get caught up into things that are toxic to our mental, physical, and spiritual health. Only because the experience feels good. It is essential to your wellbeing that you not allow these experiences control the way that you see yourself or how you value your life.

Lord,

I thank you for allowing me to see me through your eyes and yours alone. Each day that you give me breath, I thank you that I will never take it for granted. I thank you for showing me who I am in you every day. It is indeed an honor to know that no matter what I do that your love can never be separated from me.

If there is ever a point in your life that you cannot bare the hurt or the pain alone I have included some numbers of agencies that can help you through whatever you're going through. PLEASE DO NOT BE AFRAID TO USE THEM!

HELPFUL NUMBERS

National Hotlines and Helpful Links

<u>VictimConnect</u>
National Hotline for Crime Victims
1-855-4-VICTIM (1-855-484-2846)

<u>Office for Victims of Crime, Directory of Crime Victim Services</u>
[links to programs and services available to crime victims]

<u>National Suicide Prevention Lifeline</u>

1-800-273-TALK (8255) [24/7 hotline]
1-888-628-9454 (Spanish)
1-800-799-4889 (TTY)

<u>1in6 Online Helpline</u>: **A helpline for Male Survivors of Childhood Sexual Abuse and Adult Sexual Assault [24/7, free, anonymous]**

1in6 Online Support Groups: Support Groups for Male Survivors of Childhood Sexual Abuse and Adult Sexual Assault [free, anonymous]

Disaster Distress Helpline [24/7 hotline]
1-800-985-5990

FINRA Securities Helpline for Seniors
844-57-HELPS

Gift from Within (Not a hotline. A helpful link for survivors of trauma and victimization)
207.236.8858

Identity Theft Resource Center
1-888-400-5530

Internet Crime Complaint Center

Jennifer Ann's Group
Free resources on teen dating violence

MADD (Mothers Against Drunk Driving)
1-800-438-6233

National Alliance on Mental Illness

1-800-950-6264

National Association of Crime Victim Compensation Boards
[links to every state's compensation program]

National Center on Elder Abuse

National Child Abuse Hotline
1-800-422-4453

National Coalition of Anti-Violence Programs, National Advocacy for Local LGBT Communities
1-212-714-1141
[links to local programs]

National Council for Aging Care

National Domestic Violence Hotline
1-800-799-7233 or 1-800-787-3224 (TTY)

National Indigenous Women's Resource Center
406-477-3896

National Runaway Switchboard
1-800-786-2929

National Sexual Assault Hotline
1-800-656-4673 [24/7 hotline]
[hosts an online hotline]

National Teen Dating Abuse Helpline
1-866-331-9474 or 1-866-331-8453 (TTY)

Overseas Citizens Services
1-888-407-4747
1-202-501-4444 (from overseas)

Parents of Murdered Children
1-888-818-7662

Stalking Resource Center

The Trevor Project – Crisis & Suicide Prevention
Lifeline for LGBTQ Youth
1-866-488-7386

Women's Law
[information on orders of protection

Your Story Here

Lord,

          I thank you that my heart overflows with forgiveness. Forgiving everyone that has caused me any pain in my life. I thank you that as I forgive the lighter, my heart will become. Help me not to cause harm to anyone else due to the pain that has been put upon me. If I have caused anyone pain that I am made aware of it and instantly ask for forgiveness.

LET GO OF THE SECRETS AND THE GUILT

Sometimes we seem to hide behind the things that have hurt or damaged us. Instead of dealing with the issues at hand we take these feelings and suppress them. Pushing them deep down inside of us and begin piling the issues of life on top of them. It's time for you to let go of all the guilt and the secrets. Today I challenge you to take the time out to deal with these issues. They are not going to feel good coming out but remember God wants you whole.

Lord,

Thank you that all things are being made new in our lives every day. I thank you that everything that we have ever faced is up under your precious blood. As we move forward in you letting all the hurt go, we thank you that we see you in all things. You said that you would not give us more than we could bare, so we are thanking you in advance for our release.

Made in the USA
Coppell, TX
11 May 2022